Fun Dog Days

True Tales of Funny Dog Experiences

Leroy Vincent

Copyright © 2016. All rights reserved.

No part of this publication may be reproduced, stored in a retrieval system or transmitted in any way by any means, electronic, mechanical, photocopy, recording or otherwise, without the prior permission of the author except as provided by USA copyright law.

All characters appearing in this work are fictitious. Any resemblance to real persons, living or dead, is purely coincidental.

The opinions expressed by the author are not necessarily those of Revival Waves of Glory Books & Publishing.

Published by Revival Waves of Glory Books & Publishing

PO Box 596 I Litchfield, Illinois 62056 USA

www.revivalwavesofgloryministries.com

Revival Waves of Glory Books & Publishing is committed to excellence in the publishing industry.

Book design Copyright © 2016 by Revival Waves of Glory Books & Publishing. All rights reserved.

Published in the United States of America

Paperback: 978-1-68411-194-7

Table of Contents

Tale 1 1

Tale 2.. 2

Tale 3 3

Tale 4 4

Tale 5 6

Tale 6 7

Tale 7 11

Tale 8 12

Tale 9 13

Tale 10 14

Tale 11 16

Tale 12 17

Tale 13 19

Tale 14 21

Tale 15 22

Tale 16 23

Tale 17 24

Tale 18 27

Tale 19 29

Tale 20 30

Tale 21 31

Tale 22 33

Tale 23 34

Tale 24 35

Tale 25 36

Tale 26 37

Tale 27 38

Tale 28 39

Tale 29 41

Tale 30 43

Tale 31 45

Tale 32 48

Tale 33 49

Tale 1

Fritz was our dog for many years. We got him from the humane society the day he was to be put down. They told us that after we had picked him out and adopted him. Fritz loved to go camping and over time he seemed to understand the word. At the mention of going camping, he would get very excited and run through the house with a momentum that caused him to run up the kitchen cabinet face. It was really funny to watch, but we ended up having to spell camping out in order to prepare the trip.

Tale 2

I have a German Shepherd who is almost three years old and weighs a hundred pounds. One of the funniest things he does is when he is trying to find someone. If you are in a room or the hall and stand very still for about a minute, he will come to look at you, then stop and start to step back a little. If you continue to stand still, he will run away but come right back and get low to the ground while he tries to decide if he should stay or run. If you twitch or step forward, he jumps and runs away as fast as he can. Taser will run across the couch and back to you and the running starts again. You can freeze more than once and he will freak out each time. He makes a mess of the couch but he is so funny! For him it is like trying not to look at an accident, he has to come back for more!

Tale 3

My dog is a 10lb Chihuahua that is incredibly lovable and sweet but she can be a goofball too. One time, she heard something on the TV that sounded like a high pitch "I love you" and it made her react by howling/barking. So we started to mimic what she heard by howling "I love you" to see what she would do and she howled back "I love you" and got all excited. She does it every time now and it's the funniest thing ever.

Tale 4

My dog's name is Rahul. He is really good looking and very smart like Google; ideal for guarding my house. He is also very active. I remember one incident which really makes me laugh now. One time, my uncle had taken some sweet candies to eat without anyone's knowledge and hide them in his pants pocket. Actually he was a diabetic patient, so he was not supposed to eat sweet items and so he done so. The kids began to search for it and then I too began to look for the candy. It was really strange the sweet candies were missing and I began to ask the other people inside the home, but nobody seemed to have them. Suddenly my Rahul jumped towards my uncle and nipped the pocket of my uncle's pants which hardly bite his thigh and hurt him. This incident made everybody laugh.

Tale 5

I have a pet dog. Its name is Chippu and it is very naughty. Chippu plays with our children and running with them also. Every now and then, he catches the ball but he is always the winner. We like our Chippu well and he looks after the house perfectly. Frequently, it quarrels with the outdoor cats and starts barking.

Tale 6

I choose to inherit a puppy about three years ago. He is a Rhodesian Ridgeback/Rottweiler mix. When I went to pick him out of the litter of eight, all the puppies were running around and playing. As I was about to make my choice, there was this one kinda hiding behind a shrub all timid and avoiding the other puppies. I thought, hmmm cool, I like a timid dog and thought ok he would be easy to train. I went over picked him up, all cute and cuddly in his way with that nice puppy smell. I had just picked my new dog.

Moving forward about five months, training is going well. He is smart as a lick and behaves very well. I have kennel trained him since I had him and he seems to have picked up on good habits.

Now he is potty trained and not chewing on things while I am not around. So I decided let's give him a try being alone all day. I'll block off areas of the house so he only has a small place to roam. I put up all loose ends and put plenty of toys out for him to play with.

I leave for the day keeping my fingers crossed that maybe there might be one accident or he may chew up his bed. I go to work and think maybe I should go home for lunch to check on him. It's only been about four hours since I left him.

I pull up to my house and I can see him sitting on the couch all happy. As I get to the front door, I can see though the window and I was in shock as to what I saw. So I open the door and what I find is my front room of my house has been turned into a tornado zone. I mean this little dog has decided to chew every seat cushion into a thousand pieces, my coffee table looks like a corn on the cob with all the edges chewed off all the way around it. There are about five dumps on the floor. The bedroom door somehow was open and underwear, toilet paper and my down comforter was torn to shreds with feathers everywhere. I mean it looked like the Tasmanian devil went through my place and had a field day.

All the while, I see smoke and a burning smell is coming from the kitchen. I'm like what the heck is that. I go to the kitchen and one of my burners is turned on with a flame blasting out, because it is a gas stove top. For the life of me, I know I didn't leave it on because I didn't cook that morning.

After turning off the burner and going back to the living room, my puppy looks cute and all and hasn't moved from the couch where he has that I just f'd u look on his cute little face as he lay there with his head between his two front paws.

I proceeded to clean up everything which took about two hours to do. I said to myself, I really wish I had a camera in my house because all I can picture is this dog doing all of this and stopping every now and then to look in the camera as if to say, "Look daddy, if you leave me alone this is what I'm going to do for you!"

To this day I still can't for the life of me figure out how the heck he turned on the gas stove and opened my door. Needless to say my dog has grown up and is very well behaved, but it took sometime before I left him alone again. Oh, and I still don't have a coffee table.

Tale 7

My sister and I ordered pizza for lunch one day. We decided that we needed to go outside for a minute, I can't remember why, but as soon as we got outside we heard a loud crash coming from the dining room where we had left the pizza. We ran inside to find our dog, an Irish Wolfhound/German Shepard mix, sitting in the middle of the table scarfing down our pizza. She tried to hide behind the boxes when she saw us and couldn't seem to figure out if she was better off staying on the table or jumping off and hiding elsewhere. I couldn't even yell at her I was laughing so hard.

Tale 8

We are proud to announce that our 2016 tour schedule is our busiest yet! In fact, we have broken all records for the most stunt dog shows produced in one year, by one organization. As a family owned entertainment company this is a dream year! Not only are we entertaining millions in over 50 cities in the U.S., we are bringing a positive awareness of responsible pet ownership and pet adoption to each community we perform. This is our ultimate goal and passion which started back in 1999!

Tale 9

I have a border collie who really enjoys messing up rugs. One day, I yelled at him about messing up the rug by the front door. I went out and got the mail and came back to find the rug GONE. He had hiked the rug like a football player to the other side of the house to the master bedroom and put it on the other side of the bed so it was hard to find. I swear he thought it was funny. Goofball.

Tale 10

Our dog Bailee Boo is a Golden Retriever, Black Lab and German shepherd mix. She is a very special dog to us. She has a wonderful personality. She loves to lie upside down and smile. She shakes both paws, high fives, and sits pretty and will sneeze.

She loves lollipops. One day, she came with us in the SUV and we had to run into the store for something and left her in the car with it running. One of the kids had bought a bunch of these natural-flavored strawberry suckers. We get back in the car and we hear this sucking noise, and I turned around and said, "Bailee" and she popped her head up from the back seat with a sucker hanging out of her mouth. She was sucking on it. It was so funny to see her with it hanging out of her mouth! She loves them. She loves Halloween because of the lollipops.

She was run over by a big SUV when she was five months old and the vet said he had never seen a dog with such will to live and be so loyal to her family. She had a dislocated hip, bruised uterus and internal bleeding, broken ribs, etc. She was on oxygen for three days and survived it all.

Tale 11

I have a three year old Alaskan malamute. When I lived in Washington, I had a sliding glass door and I had left my dog in the house in order to do yard work. I looked at the sliding glass door and she is in the middle of opening the sliding glass door by nudging the handle with her nose. She finally got it open and out she came.

Tale 12

My dog, Snow, is both deaf and blind, so besides his playfulness and affection, he can be a little harder to deal with than other dogs. His sense of smell is even more impressive and prominent than an ordinary dogs as it's his primary way of getting to grips with the world around him. Plus, when it comes to food and treats, he knows that if he can smell it then he has to sit calmly in a specific way before he'll be given it.

A few months ago my brother came to stay for a few weeks, and other than what I'd cook, his diet seemed to consist almost solely of toast or peanut butter sandwiches. Now, Snow, like most dogs, absolutely loves peanut butter, and despite my brother having never shared any with him, Snow quickly got into the habit of going to him and sitting to get a treat. I can only imagine that my brother smelled faintly enough of peanut butter for his stay, because without fail Snow would start to sit and beg every time my brother entered the same room as him.

    My brother came over again last weekend too. My partner let him in and forgot to let me know, but when I got in after a walk, the dog tipped me off before anyone else. Still thinking my brother must have been made of peanut butter and having got one whiff of him, the dog rushed upstairs and sat outside the spare room where my brother was ready to get a treat.

Tale 13

The best dog I ever had weighed 12lbs and he was a terrier mix named Tuffy. He got the name because he thought he was the biggest, baddest dog that ever lived.

The neighborhood that we lived in had a lot of cats and as dogs do they chase cats. Of course, Tuffy made himself the sheriff of our yard and "no cats were allowed". One day as Tuffy was making his rounds in the yard, he came across a big tom cat that he immediately began to bark at and run after. The cat, which was at least 2-3 times bigger than Tuffy, did not run like the other cats. Instead he turned and began chasing the dog.

After the incident when it was time for Tuffy to use the bathroom, he would stick his head out the door and look around like he was making sure it was safe before going outside.

It was so funny, needless to say he never chased another cat, he moved on to birds.

Tale 14

When we first got our puppy she was scared of everything. I can remember a pillow falling and landing upright and roughly looking like the shape of a small child and her standing there barking at it for at least five minutes.

Tale 15

My dog Rambo is so funny. He is about five pounds and thinks he weighs a hundred. We love it when he growls because it is so loud and vicious and makes a gurgle sound. And to hear it coming from his little body makes us laugh so hard we almost pee ourselves.

Our children love to play wrestle with us and the funniest thing is that Rambo is very over protective of them and when he sees us wrestling he starts to 'attack' and he thinks he is doing something with his little self and we all fall out in a fit of laughter!

Tale 16

A dog is recovering after managing to cling to the grille of a car for almost 60 miles. The dog travelled all the way from Coleraine to Belfast, wedged in the front of a Peugeot 306.

The driver thought he had struck something on the dual carriageway outside Coleraine after hearing a thud, but when he saw nothing on the road, he continued unaware of his 'passenger'. It was only when he got out at the Odyssey Arena in Belfast that he heard a barking sound coming from the front bonnet.

After such an ordeal, the dog was understandably grumpy, and this attitude has earned him the nickname Father Jack, in honor of the cantankerous priest in the sitcom Father Ted as reported by Peter Allen on Radio 5 Live 'Drive' program.

Tale 17

Describing a dog can be a very fun filled writing exercise. Almost everyone loves dogs and that always shines through in an assignment on our canine friends. There are three different levels in this post. Level 1 is in Basic English and it goes up to Level 3 which is Intermediate English. The grids are to be read downwards but it may be easier just to pluck out any words you find useful and mix them up for your essay. If you are a student, I hope this helps you with your assignment. God bless for now and take care.

We own a handbag dog. At least that is what my mother calls her, probably because she takes her shopping in her handbag. She is a miniature Yorkshire terrier and she is a delight. Her most attractive quality is that she is friendly to everyone, especially children.

They love her molten-brown eyes and her glossy fur. She also has the cutest little paws. They are like a fox's paws and she loves to dig up the garden with them. She also has a small, marshmallow tail. It is soft and white so we just call it the marshmallow.

She can be very ladylike and fussy about her food at times. She turns her nose up at dog food but would snap your hand off for a chocolate digestive. Her small, sharp teeth make short work of any treats we give her.

She is always playful and that is why we adore her. Her whip-thin body is very energetic. I'm sure she believes she's a gazelle or a cheetah at times! Although she can be as temperamental as a human child, we wouldn't swop her for anything.

Labradors are such a contrary bunch. Yes, they're cuddly and playful but I find that there's a dark side to them sometimes. My guy, Elvis, will be lying by the fire on a winter's night dreaming his doggy dreams when suddenly out of nowhere, he will emit a bloodcurdling growl. He looks like Cujo when he does that, with his teeth bared and the hackles rising on his neck. I often wonder if he is chasing an imaginary rabbit or a burglar when he's dreaming. Maybe it's just the last remnants of wolfdog coming to the surface. He's never exhibited aggression towards me but it would make one think all the same.

When he switches back to Labrador mode, he is quite the character. His eyes become mellow and warm again and they glow with a lagoon-blue sheen. He has great physical qualities also. His fur is burnished, almost coppery, and he bounces along with energy on those soft pads of his. Blessed with a streamlined tail for balance, he is the most hyperactive and agile dog I've ever befriended.

Tale 18

I have a two year old Boxer. It's brown and white, and it's extremely intelligent and funny. Once I was outside my house with a friend and my dog, we were talking about stuff and the dog was running around barking at every person he saw, and he was even barking at other dogs or cats passing by.

He is a loyal dog and he always sits next to me as if he is guarding me. Suddenly, I couldn't see or hear my dog but I continued talking to my friend who was sitting on the curb. Then I felt something warm on my back, and I turned around and I saw that my dog had been peeing on my back like marking his territory. My friend laughed a lot for a long time and I got very embarrassed and mad at my dog for doing that.

I went back into my house and my mom, brother and sister were laughing too because they saw my t-shirt wet and very smelly, so they referred to me as a dog's toilet tree. Then I stopped being mad and I started laughing with my friend and family. What a moment to remember. What a dog!

Tale 19

Sometimes my dog with take possession of a shoe or a dish towel, or some other household item. This is the only time he is ever mean, and he growls at us. However, we yell, "Get in your room!" which is the laundry room where his bed and toys are and he will run to "his room", snarling the whole way there as if he is an angry teenager!

Tale 20

My dog's name is PotPie and she is a Golden Lab. I lived alone when I got her so when I went to work she had to be left alone. She was far too active, really, to be alone, and one day I came home to find my entire couch ripped up with her laying on top of it as if nothing had happened. I took a picture of her at that moment, and today it is my favorite picture. The expression on her face was one of total denial, and she was laying there as if she had finally gotten the couch comfortable for her.

Tale 21

I have a Jack Russell/Chihuahua mix named Daisy. Something funny that she does is her attempts to jump up onto the bed. I pat my bed for her to hop up and she attempts to run and jump and bounces off the edge of the bed and back to the floor. She does this about three or four times before she runs towards the bed and actually makes it on top of the bed.

I also have a cat. One time, when the cat was a baby, I had her up on the bed and Daisy walked into my room. I called her up and she attempted to hop up like normal and when she finally made it, she realized the cat was on the bed. They both froze and stared at one another. The hair on Daisy's neck stood up a bit, as she was getting playful. Suddenly, my cat hopped towards her and it scared Daisy and she stepped back and fell off the bed. She didn't hurt herself and when she tried to hop back up, that ended up scaring the cat. They both scared each other and it was funny to witness.

Tale 22

My dog, Jake, and I went for a walk in the park. This park has specified areas for horses and they will go on the same trails that people walk on. When Jake first saw the horses, he looked at them like they were huge dogs. He wasn't too sure about the horses. At first, he walked sideways near them but then got the courage to actually go up to one and sniff him. The horse lowered his head to smell Jake as well. It seems that the two were getting along just great and then the horse let out a big sneeze all over Jake. It was hysterical to watch his reaction to the sneeze. That experience still makes me laugh when I think of it.

Today, Jake still likes horses and wants to go up to every one of them and say, "Hello".

Tale 23

My dog is a short and round Corgi Labrador that loves to candy. His favorite is suckers. One day, he came with us in the pickup and while we ran in the store for something we left him in the car with it running. My son had bought a bunch of these natural-flavored strawberry suckers. We get back in the truck and we hear this sucking noise, and I turned around and said, "Reggie" and he popped his head up from the back seat with a sucker hanging out of his mouth.

Tale 24

My dog is a German shepherd, Beagle, Dachshund mix. This type of mutt makes for a cute Beagle sized dog with a lot of energy.

She's been hit by a car twice. As a result, and probably as a result of watching us humans, she now sits on her butt like a human with one leg splayed out. She even allows her legs to dangle rather than sitting on their hinds like most dogs do. It still hits a comical bone when I see her sitting on any stoop like a human. She even sits on the porch looking out at the sunset with her tail flat against the deck wood.

Tale 25

My dog loves to chew on things as most dogs do. What makes my dog so funny is the way he loves to chew on his toys or his bones, and basically whatever he can get his paws on. So imagine a toy poodle lying on his back, his front paws hugging a bone that mind you is for a dog that is the size of a German Shepard, just chomping away.

All you have to do to see how happy a boy he is, call his name as you walk up to him while he has a chew toy. It brings a smile to my face but whatever you do don't think about taking that bone away...then the chase is on!

Tale 26

I was having friends over so about an hour before they arrived, I took my dog on a walk to let him do his business. After the walk, I get showered and dressed. I come out and he is scooting around on my wood floors with his front paws, dragging his rear end. He had smeared feces all over my living room. Right then, my door bell rings and my friends were there.

Tale 27

I had a puppy that I just got from the humane society. This was the most precious little puppy in the world. I took him home and he slept with me like a little baby.

The first day I went to work and came home all of my shoes and clothes were in rags. That is not the best part. The next day, this puppy grabbed my false teeth off of my nightstand and ran out and buried them in the back yard. So I woke up and did not see my false teeth and had to go in the backyard and dig them up and wash them off. But I only found the top half and not the bottom. I hurried up and washed them of and threw them in my mouth and went to work with only the top teeth and no bottom teeth.

Tale 28

I was playing fetch with my newly adopted, nine year-old Jack Russel Terrier, Cooper, in my fenced-in backyard. The neighbor let his dog out in his back yard. Neither dog had been in contact with one another before. The neighbor's dog was a little fluffy Bichon Frise named Snickers. My dog spots the neighbor's dog and runs over to him in a flash. My dog runs under my chain-link fence as if the fence didn't even exist and begins attacking the neighbor's dog.

I cannot get to my dog because the fence is in the way.

My neighbor runs over and kicks my dog off of his dog. My dog lets out a squeal and is distracted from the attack. The neighbor grabs his dog and runs him back into the house.

After I got my dog back into my house, I went over to apologize for my dog's behavior but my knocks at the door were ignored. Fortunately, I later found out that his dog was not injured.

My dog now has to be taken out on a leash each time despite having a fenced-in back yard since it just cannot contain him.

Tale 29

Several years ago, I gave piano lessons in my home. The room where I gave lessons had easy access from the front door. Students came in the front door and we had privacy from the other parts of the house. There was a bi-fold door that divided this room and the room next to it.

My family had a dog, Arnie, who was rather unpredictable. The one thing I could normally predict was that he would be in the other part of the house while I gave lessons.

I was attentively giving piano lessons to a teenage student and all of a sudden I smelled a familiar, yet pungent odor. I know I had not expelled gas and I was pretty sure my student hadn't. I was beginning to feel very embarrassed.

Out of the corner of my eye, I saw something furry and black and white. Somehow my dog had pushed the bi-fold door open without me seeing and had hidden behind a chair. Or should I say, he pooped behind the chair. This was very out of character for him. My dog left the room and I sat there not knowing what to do. Part of me wanted to say something and part of me wanted to act as if I couldn't smell anything. I didn't know whether to clean the mess up or let it go until my student left. My student never said anything so maybe her sense of smell wasn't as good as mine.

Tale 30

"My Westie, Dash, lifted his leg and peed on a pile of ladies' purses at my husband's 50th birthday party," said Amy Weirick. The party was held in the backyard, and in Dash's defense, the purses were thrown in a pile under a tree. "His favorite tree, apparently."

Another time, Weirick was walking Dash past the elementary school during her 10-year-old son's lacrosse practice. The kids came over to the shade of a tree, where their thermos-type water jugs had been placed. "Just as the coach and his son approached, Dash lifted his leg and let lose all over the top of the coach's kid's water bottle," Weirick said. She took the bottle home, scrubbed it, bleached it and returned it to the boy. "Bottom line: In our dog's eyes, anything left under a tree is fair game for leaving his mark."

Tale 31

I recently got a bad haircut. I was embarrassed. In fact, it happened the day before I had to emcee a very well-attended charity event. I wasn't happy but I soldiered on, blushing the entire night. The reason I mention this is because of a complaint I heard from a client recently. She had taken her dog to her groomer (not one of ours, thankfully) and reported that her dog's hair was cut so short her pooch acted embarrassed. She shared how her dog ran inside from the car and immediately hid under the bed after her "bad haircut." She wouldn't come out for several hours, even when her husband came home and offered her a treat.

Do dogs get embarrassed if they have a "bad hair" day? I'd never really given it much thought. Turns out some canine behavior researchers have. Dr. Marc Bekoff, a former professor of ecology and evolutionary biology at the University of Colorado and author of "The Emotional Lives of Animals," has observed dogs for thousands of hours in his career. He concludes that dogs do have feelings of "embarrassment, shyness and humiliation."

Another researcher, neurobiologist Dr. Frederick Range at the University of Vienna, agrees. His studies demonstrate that dogs have other secondary emotions such as "jealousy, guilt and empathy."

I'm guessing Markoff and Range would definitely agree with my client that her close-cropped canine was most certainly "embarrassed."

Not every animal behavior expert agrees. In fact, most say researchers such as Markoff and Range are missing a few synapses when they talk about dogs having complex emotions such as embarrassment (you don't want to know what they say about me). The traditional notion is dogs only experience "instant-reaction" emotions such as fear, joy, sadness and anger. Established thought would state embarrassment is far beyond the emotional reach of dogs.

I'd love for them to meet my menagerie and still believe that. Not only do I believe my dogs feel secondary emotions, they're also capable of being downright silly. Study that, superstar know-it-all experts.

In my own experience posing as "Santa Paws" for nineteen years and witnessing an almost endless parade of dressed-up and dolled-up dogs and cats, I can tell you some pets are clearly unhappy with what mom and dad are doing to them.

Tale 32

My husband, my son, and I went to the airport to pick up family friends for the holidays. They aren't the biggest fans of dogs, but I reassured them that our dog was really well behaved and always road in the car. So about five minutes down the road, after having picked them up, we heard a loud fart, and my son start to laugh saying, "Reggie farted." All of a sudden the whole car stunk and we had to roll down the windows to try to air it out quick. To say the least those family friends never asked for a ride again.

Tale 33

Last week over the holiday, my entire family was sitting at the dining room table eating lunch. We had a typical holiday meal of turkey, potatoes, gravy, vegetables, and dessert. Meanwhile, we were all unaware that in the kitchen, my dog was doing something absolutely funny. My dog, whose name is Axl (named after the singer Axl Rose), was sitting on the counter and eating a meal of his own. As my wife turned the corner to get some more gravy for the mashed potatoes, she saw him leap off of the counter top and run down into the basement. Unfortunately for us, the gravy has all been eaten by Axl.

For the next few hours, Axl spent time in the basement and my entire family laughed about the experience. I wondered if the gravy would make him sick, and my grandpa wondered if the gravy would make him vomit. In the end, Axl did not get sick and he never did vomit. I am sure, however, that this funny dog story will stick with my family at family gatherings for years and generations to come.

Be sure to get your copy of Fun Dog Days Coloring Book.

www.ingramcontent.com/pod-product-compliance
Lightning Source LLC
Chambersburg PA
CBHW052120070526
44584CB00017B/2574